GEARED FOR GROWTH BIBLE STUDIES
ENTERING BY FAITH
A STUDY IN HEBREWS

BIBLE STUDIES TO IMPACT THE LIVES OF ORDINARY PEOPLE

Written by Marie Dinnen

The Word Worldwide

CHRISTIAN FOCUS

For details of our titles visit us on our website
www.christianfocus.com

ISBN 1-85792-914-4

Copyright © WEC International

Published in 2003 by
Christian Focus Publications, Geanies House,
Fearn, Ross-shire, IV20 ITW, Scotland
and
WEC International, Bulstrode, Oxford Road,
Gerrards Cross, Bucks, SL9 8SZ

Cover design by Alister MacInnes

Printed and bound by J W Arrowsmith, Bristol

CONTENTS

PREFACE 4
INTRODUCTORY STUDY 5

QUESTIONS AND NOTES

STUDY 1 – 'BETTER THAN ANGELS' 7
STUDY 2 – WASN'T MOSES THE GREATEST PROPHET? 9
STUDY 3 – GREATEST OF ALL 11
STUDY 4 – GROWING UP! 13
STUDY 5 – KING AND PRIEST – PERFECT AND ETERNAL 15
STUDY 6 – THE TRUE TABERNACLE AND THE NEW COVENANT 18
STUDY 7 – JESUS THE NEW AND LIVING WAY 21
STUDY 8 – 'NOW FAITH IS BEING SURE ...' (NIV) 23
STUDY 9 – A FAITH THAT FUNCTIONS AND NEVER GIVES UP 26
STUDY 10 29

ANSWER GUIDE

STUDY 1 35
STUDY 2 36
STUDY 3 37
STUDY 4 38
STUDY 5 39
STUDY 6 40
STUDY 7 41
STUDY 8 42
STUDY 9 43
STUDY 10 44

PREFACE
GEARED FOR GROWTH

**'Where there's LIFE there's GROWTH:
Where there's GROWTH there's LIFE.'**

WHY GROW a study group?

Because as we study the Bible and share together we can

- learn to combat loneliness, depression, staleness, frustration, and other problems
- get to understand and love each other
- become responsive to the Holy Spirit's dealing and obedient to God's Word

and that's GROWTH.

How do you GROW a study group?

- Just start by asking a friend to join you and then aim at expanding your group.
- Study the set portions daily (they are brief and easy: no catches).
- Meet once a week to discuss what you find.
- Befriend others, both Christians and non Christians, and work away together

see how it GROWS!

WHEN you GROW ...

This will happen at school, at home, at work, at play, in your youth group, your student fellowship, women's meetings, mid-week meetings, churches and communities,

you'll be REACHING THROUGH TEACHING

INTRODUCTORY STUDY

'Well, if Bill is a Christian, I'm not interested. I reckon the life I live is as good as his any day.'

'Anne says you've got to go to church at least once every Sunday, and on special church-days too. If you do that, you're O.K. But even she admits she finds it boring.'

'We gave Craig the works the other day! Teased him for being so religious. I mean, it's not natural, this "holier-than-thou" thing – so now he says he'll join the gang and give up his queer ideas.'

Discuss the above statement by non-Christians. Have you ever heard people expressing any of these opinions? Where do Bill, Anne and Craig fall down? Do you find any of these are areas of temptation for you?

If we are honest with ourselves, we'll realize that we don't always live the way our Lord wants us to. It's so easy to give way to our natural feelings and think, 'Well, that's just me. I can't help it.'

In the first century AD, things were very similar. Ordinary people like you and me became Christians, rejoiced in the resources available to them in Jesus Christ, then lost their initial enthusiasm by becoming bogged down with ritual, doubt or pressure from the world. It is to these people (Jews) that the letter to the Hebrews was written.

Look up the following references and discuss areas where people could go wrong:

Hebrews 2:1 and 13:9; 3:6 and 10:32-35; 3:12; 5:11; 5:12-14; 10:25; 12:3, 12; 13:17

Does all this sound familiar?

The letter we are going to study deals with these problems, and gives the answer – JESUS CHRIST Himself. We shall find that we are encouraged not to give up, but to hold fast our faith and grow in the knowledge and love of God.

A good summary of the letter is given at the beginning of Hebrews in the Good News Bible.

Read Hebrews 1:1-3 together. Share any incidents in the Bible you can think of, where God spoke prior to the coming of Christ.

Look up Romans 1:20 and then discuss these points: How does creation speak to us about God? What does nature portray about God's character? What does it convey about our relationship with God?

Look at Hebrews 1:2 again, and discuss how God most effectively communicates with us, and what He tells us by this means.

Read Hebrews 1:1-3 (if possible in the Living Bible). These are some of the most important verses in the Bible. Share them in as many versions are you can.

What is the key verse to Hebrews? ... Chapter 4:14. See if you can learn this by heart before next week.

'God has spoken to His people' – we only communicate with one another when we have something to say. Do you believe God has something to say to you today? And in the days ahead when you study this book? Be sure you listen for His voice.

God has spoken! ... By degrees and in different ways!

In Old Testament times He did so through dreams, visions, judgments, deliverances, the law, the ordinances, through men and the word of prophecy. The human beings He used were at best imperfect. But now ... God has spoken through His Son! ... Perfectly, finally, through the perfect God-Man!

In the New Testament, particularly in the first three verses of Hebrews we get a clear picture of God's unfolding plan of salvation fulfilled in Christ. He is the supreme revelation of God to us. He is King. He is Prophet. He is the Great High Priest. He is the Creator and Controller of the Universe.

What happens when the postman calls at your house? A letter? Who from? What's it all about? Aren't we eager to tear open the envelope and find out?

Let's get Hebrews out of the envelope. It's from God. It's all about His Son. We are not told which human hand wrote it – but the printer only puts down what the head dictates! The letter warns us against bondage to custom and legalism. It shows us the better way to a right relationship with God. It shows us better, no – the best things that God has provided for us, both in time and eternity through Christ. Chapters 1-9 are teaching ones, the rest of the book shows us how to make the teaching practical in our experience.

This letter or book was written for early Jewish Christians, but its message is for us today. If we read, accept and apply its teaching we shall learn how to walk in the new and better way – in Christ.

STUDY 1

'BETTER THAN ANGELS'

QUESTIONS

DAY 1 *Hebrews 1:4-14.*
a) List what God says about angels here.
b) List what He says about His Son.
c) What does the comparison show you?

DAY 2 Read these Hebrews verses and the corresponding Old Testament ones:
Hebrews 1:5 and Psalm 2:7.
Hebrews 1:8, 9 and Psalm 45:6, 7.
Hebrews 1:6 and Psalm 97:7.
Hebrews 1:10-12 and Psalm 102:25-27.
Hebrews 1:7 and Psalm 104:4.
Hebrews 1:13 and Psalm 110:1.
a) What does this tell you about the God of the Old and New Testament?
b) In what other ways can you show the truth of Hebrews 13:8?

DAY 3 *Hebrews 1:14–2:4.*
a) To whom were God's messengers sent?
b) What does God say to us (2:3)?

DAY 4 *Read Hebrews 2:1-4 in several versions if possible.*
a) What conclusion is drawn about our responsibility since we live after Christ came?
b) In what three ways are we shown that the message of salvation is true?

DAY 5 *Hebrews 2:5-8.*
a) Will angels rule in Heaven?
b) What do verses 7 and 8 say about man's intended authority?

DAY 6 *Hebrews 2:9-15; Psalm 51.*
a) What do you think is meant by Jesus having been made a little lower than the angels (v. 9)?
b) Why did Jesus have to die?
c) What does the Psalmist teach us about the way to forgiveness?

DAY 7 *Hebrews 2:10-18; John 17:11.*
From these verses, list and discuss some of the benefits we have from Christ's sacrifice.

NOTES

The King James Version of Scripture in verse 5 of Chapter 1, uses the term 'begotten Son'.

This term emphasizes the uniqueness of Jesus and as such the Angels, God's created beings, must worship Christ (v. 6) and care for those whom He redeems (v. 14).

But Jesus, born of Mary, by the Holy Spirit (Matt. 1:18) is the Son of God, the perfect God-Man. This gives the lie to the teaching of Jehovah's Witnesses that Christ was the highest created Angel.

The Genesis story reveals how much man lost through disobedience and sin (Gen. 1). The Hebrews story shows how the God-Man redeemed us, restoring our lost inheritance. How? His victory at Calvary has put 'everything under His feet' in heaven and on earth (Heb. 2:8) and being made new creatures in Him, we become joint heirs in His inheritance (Rom. 8:17).

The law with its binding and ritual, is done away with in Christ. The basis of our acceptance by God is whether we are IN the perfect LAWKEEPER – Christ Himself – or not (2 Cor. 5:17) and whether His standards are now kept in our hearts (2 Cor. 3:3).

In the old Roman culture ANGELS were regarded as DEMI-GODS.

In Jewish days the HIGH PRIEST stood between GOD AND MAN.

Now, we have a GREAT HIGH PRIEST who continually lives to intercede for US. Christ is our LIVING WAY into the presence of God.

We lost out in Adam, but...

- where we fell into the bondage of sin, Christ RELEASES US FROM THIS SLAVERY (Heb. 2:14, 15).
- where we lost our relationship with God, CHRIST MAKES US ONE WITH HIM (Heb. 2:10-13).
- where we were robbed of our spiritual inheritance, Christ RESTORES THAT INHERITANCE AGAIN (Heb. 2:5-9).

STUDY 2

WASN'T MOSES THE GREATEST PROPHET?

QUESTIONS

DAY 1 *Hebrews 3:1-6.*
a) What do you think is meant by God's house? (See also Isa. 66:1, 2; Exod. 35:1-19; 1 Chron. 17:11-15; Acts 17:24.)
b) Who is building God's house?

DAY 2 *Hebrews 3:5, 6; Ephesians 3:17.*
a) What is the difference between a servant and a son?
b) Between Moses and Christ?
c) What are the conditions we must fulfil, if we are to be His dwelling-place?

DAY 3 *Hebrews 3:7-17.*
a) Discuss the incident in the Moses story to which this refers (Num. 13 and 14:1-23).
b) Why do you think the Israelites reacted as they did?
c) What word is emphasized by repetition in these verses?

DAY 4 *Hebrews 3:18, 19; Numbers 13:31-33.*
a) What did the Israelites expect life to be like in God's Promised Land?
b) What made them afraid?
c) What really kept them out of Canaan?

DAY 5 *Hebrews 4:1-4; Ephesians 2:14, 15; Matthew 11:29; Hebrews 4:11.*
a) What does God offer us?
b) What can hinder us from having it?

DAY 6 *Hebrews 4:5-11; Psalm 95:8; Exodus 8:32; Exodus 10:1; Genesis 6:3.*
a) Pick out two warnings in verses 5-11.
b) Put into your own words what you think a hard heart is.

DAY 7 *Hebrews 4:11-14.*
a) What personal advice are we given here?
b) Discuss:
  i. Why Christ is greater than Moses. (John 1:1)
  ii. The power of the Word of God. (Exod. 14:13; Eph. 6:17)

NOTES

What have we seen about Moses?
A man, conscious of weaknesses, dependent on God, human, faithful, capable of disobedience, God's leader of Israel, lawgiver under God's direction, a member of God's household, a foreshadow of Christ.

What have we seen about Christ?
God incarnate, perfect man, perfectly obedient, embodiment of the law of God, Master builder of God's house and much, much more.
(See Acts 17:24; Rev. 21:3; 1 Cor. 6:19; Eph. 3:17, 19)

What have we learned about Moses' task?
He was to lead Israel out of bondage in Egypt into God's land of promise.

What have we learned about Christ's task?
He came to free us from the bondage of Satan and sin and to bring us into the glorious liberty and joy of salvation.

What have we learned from Israel's failures?
That just as they failed through fear and unbelief so that some never went into Canaan, so we can miss out on the promises of God and never enter into our rightful inheritance.

See how the Israelites doubted the power (Num. 13:27-33), love (Num. 14:1-5), and Word (Num. 14:11) of God.

DANGER!   ACT NOW!   TODAY, TODAY, TODAY!

Never play about with revealed truth (1 Cor. 10:9-12; Jas. 4:14; John 3:19-20).

A TRUSTY WEAPON!
The sword of the Spirit, the Word of God, is the only and an almighty weapon against sin. We shouldn't be afraid when God uses it upon us, for He only uses it to deal with sin and bring us to blessing. David, the Psalmist, knew its effectiveness and sang: 'I have hidden your word in my heart that I might not sin against you' (Ps. 119:11). 'I will extol the LORD at all times ... I sought the Lord and he answered me; he delivered me from all my fears' (Ps. 34:1-4).

STUDY 3
GREATEST OF ALL

QUESTIONS

DAY 1 *Hebrews 4:14; 6:19, 20; 7:25.*
a) When the writer says 'we', to whom is he referring?
b) Where is our great High Priest now?
c) What are we told about Him in chapter 6, the first half of verse 20?

DAY 2 *Hebrews 4:15; Matthew 4:1-11; Isaiah 53:4.*
a) How did Christ deal with temptation?
b) How do we know that He really understands and cares about our problems?

DAY 3 *Hebrews 4:16; 1 John 1:9.*
a) How are Christians told to come into God's presence?
b) Discuss why and on what grounds we are to come?

DAY 4 *Hebrews 5:1-4; Leviticus 4:35; Leviticus 16:6.*
a) Who appointed the Old Testament (Aaronic) priest?
b) What was his job?
c) Why did he have to offer a sacrifice for himself?

DAY 5 *Hebrews 5:4-6; 2 Corinthians 5:21; Hebrews 10:12.*
a) Who appointed Christ?
b) What was His task?
c) In what ways did it differ from the work of the Aaronic priest?

DAY 6 *Hebrews 5:7-9; Luke 2:51; John 4:34; Philippians 2:8.*
a) How were the qualities of submission, obedience and humility expressed in Christ's life?
b) What can we, as God's children, expect? (Heb. 12:6-11)

DAY 7 *Hebrews 5:7-10; 2:10, 14; Luke 22:41-46; Romans 6:9; 1 Corinthians 15:44, 45; 2 Corinthians 5:21; 1 Peter 2:24.*
Read the references ...
Meditate on the thoughts your leader reads out ...
Thank God that by accepting so 'great salvation' we need never fear death.

NOTES

Our Great High Priest.
Every title given Him in Scripture bears out that He is PERFECT.

Lamb of God	Perfect, spotless sacrifice for sin (John 1:29, 36).
Messiah	Heralding a perfect salvation and perfect rule of righteousness (John 4:25).
Jesus	Perfect Saviour (Matt. 1:16, 21).
Christ	Anointed of God for a perfect work (Heb. 1:9; Acts 4:27).
Emmanuel	Embodiment of God Himself (Matt. 1:23).
Son of God	Equal with God in holiness, majesty, power, etc., (John 5:18; Phil. 2:6).
Lord	Of the universe, the Church and every living soul (Phil. 2:9-11; Rom. 14:8).
Great High Priest	Representing His people before God (Heb. 4:14).
Mediator	Middle man – the go-between us and God (Heb. 8:6 and 9:15).

Although Jesus was in no way morally imperfect YET, in order to redeem us He had to be MADE PERFECT. Thus He identified with us through His sufferings. He had to prove Himself in:

Submissiveness in His Human Relationships
He became subject to His earthly parents and commended Himself to God and man (Luke 2:51, 52).

in His Relationship with Satan
Tempted to take the devil's suggestions rather than God's way, He did not fail (Luke 4:8).

Obedience in His Relationship with God
All through His life (John 8:29).
In Gethsemane (Luke 22:42).
At Calvary (Luke 23:46).

'Ours is not a High Priest who cannot sympathize with our weaknesses, but One who was in every respect tested as we are, yet without committing sin.'
Because He Himself suffered in being tempted, He is able to bring aid to those who are tempted.

THEREFORE...
'Let us then approach the throne of grace with confidence, so that we may receive mercy and find grace to help us in our time of need' (Heb. 4:16).

STUDY 4

GROWING UP!

QUESTIONS

DAY 1 *Hebrews 5:10-14; 1 Corinthians 13:11.*
a) What two things do these verses say about (1) infants, (2) adults?
b) What spiritual lesson can we learn from verses 13 and 14?
c) Put into your own words what you think the writer means in Hebrews 5:11, 12.

DAY 2 *Hebrews 5:12; 6:1-3; 2 Corinthians 7:1; Ephesians 4:12; James 1:22; 1 John 3:2.*
a) What is there in these verses which would explain the 'elementary truths' (v. 12, NIV) and 'elementary teachings' of Christ (Heb. 6:1)?
b) Discuss God's views on Christian maturity and how we can get there.

DAY 3 *Hebrews 6:4-6; Exodus 14:30, 31; Numbers 32:10-13.*
a) Who crossed the Red Sea, and who went into Canaan?
b) What message gets through to you from verses 4-6?

DAY 4 *Hebrews 6:6-8; Luke 20:13-16; Matthew 7:16; Matthew 13:22-30; 2 Timothy 2:19; 2 Peter 1:10, 11; 2 Peter 2:1; Jude 4.*
a) In what two specific ways can people react to the truth of God's Word?
b) Discuss the result of both decisions.

DAY 5 *Hebrews 6:9-12; 1 Corinthians 13:13; Galatians 5:13.*
a) What three things are referred to in Hebrews 6:10,11?
b) What three things are referred to in 1 Corinthians 13:13?
c) What practical instructions are given in Hebrews 6:11,12?

DAY 6 *Hebrews 6:13-16; Genesis 12:1-3; 15:6; 22:16.*
a) How was God's promise to bless Abraham backed up?
b) What effect did this have on Abraham?
c) Why do people give pledges to each other?

DAY 7 *Hebrews 6:17-20; Malachi 3:6; Luke 1:71-75; Ephesians 1:17-23.*
a) What promise has God given those who obey Him?
b) What is His guarantee that He will bring this to pass?
c) What is our anchor in the storms of life?

NOTES

I'm sure every new mother eyes her baby with delight. Ten fingers! Ten toes! Eyes, nose, mouth! So dainty, so perfect! But hearts are stirred to compassion when they see a grown person who has failed to reach full development either physically or mentally.

Growth is automatic if all the cells are alive and proper nourishment provided. We don't expect to see a healthy young adult sit down to a 40g bottle of milk three times a day, any more than we would feed a new born babe on steak!

Our Hebrews' writer is obviously disappointed that these Christians are so immature that he cannot attempt to explain to them the meaning of the Melchizedek Priesthood. So he draws from the above picture to say that those who are 'born again' (John 3:3) – i.e., made totally new in Christ, should go on from the stage where they are content to enjoy the basics of salvation or are continually looking to others for spiritual food, to the place where they can get stuck into a solid diet and so mature that they can teach others (2 Tim. 2:2).

The writer then draws from another picture which is likened in 'What More Can God Say?' to a still-born child. It looks so perfect, so complete, yet there is no life. As the Israelites came near Canaan, some of them revealed their lack of faith (spiritual life?) by refusing to go in, and because of their unbelief they never got into the land. Scripture makes it clear that many so-called Christians appear to be all right, but when the final test comes God will make it clear that they haven't truly entered into spiritual life (Matt. 7:22, 23).

There is a solemn warning for those who have learned the truths of salvation yet turn their backs on God's loving gift. They are judged as those who wilfully crucify Jesus all over again (Heb. 6:6).

Encouragement is a wonderful thing! Maybe these Christians needed stirring along. Don't we all? The writer encourages them, acknowledging their FAITH in God, HOPE of eternal salvation and LOVE towards others. There are three things to spur us on too:

1. The record of God fulfilling His promises to others, e.g., Abraham (Heb. 6:14, 15).
2. God's promise and oath to us (Heb. 6:18).
3. Our living Guarantee who provides a sure anchorage (Heb. 6:19, 20; Phil. 1:6).

STUDY 5

KING AND PRIEST – PERFECT AND ETERNAL

QUESTIONS

DAY 1 *Read Hebrews 5:10, 11 again.*
a) What topic is the writer anxious to come to?
b) What are we told about Melchizedek in Genesis 14:17-20?

DAY 2 *Hebrews 7:1-3; Hebrews 8:1; 1 Timothy 1:17; Zechariah 6:13; Psalm 110:4.*
a) What do these verses say about Melchizedek?
b) Discuss the points of similarity between him and Christ.

DAY 3 *Hebrews 7:1-3; Exodus 12:17; Luke 22:19, 20.*
a) What was the significance of these feasts?
b) What do we celebrate at the Lord's table (Communion)?

DAY 4 *Hebrews 7:1, 7; Genesis 27:27-29; Ephesians 1:3-7*
a) Who is the greater, the blesser or the blessed?
b) What tremendous blessing is mentioned as given in Ephesians 1:3-7?

DAY 5 *Hebrews 7:4-10; Genesis 14:20; Genesis 28:22; Leviticus 27:30-33; Numbers 18:21-32; Luke 11:42.*
a) What prompted Abraham and Jacob to give tithes?
b) How were the Levites supported?
c) Who told Moses to instruct the people in tithing?
d) Should we tithe?

DAY 6 *Hebrews 7:11-28.*
a) What do these verses say about the law and the Levites?
b) Note who Aaron was (Exod. 4:14); his failures (Exod. 32:1-6); his sins (Lev. 4:3); the weakness of the Levitical priesthood (Lev. 21:21); Aaron's death (Num. 20:22-29) and what God said He would have to do for the house of Levi (Mal. 3:3).

QUESTIONS (contd.)

DAY 7 *Hebrews 7:8-28: especially verses 8, 21, 25, 28 (in the Living Bible, if possible).*
What words indicate that the Melchizedek priesthood is God's final answer?
(Read John 14:6 and I Tim. 2:5-6 to see what happened to the Levitical priesthood. Also, our study for Day Two shows that Melchizedek and Christ have the double office of King-Priest. Read I Pet. 2:9 and Rev. 1:5-6 and see that God says all believers become Kings and Priests too. We will study this more fully later.)

NOTES

Let's see what Hebrews tells us about it:
The priest could only approach God with an offering, both for himself and for the people. The same pattern continued over and over again:

sin
guilt
sorrow
sacrifice
forgiveness

BUT – earthly priests and ministers only pointed to the need for a 'better' way for man to come into God's eternal, holy presence.
The priests themselves were *imperfect* and *temporal*. The sacrificial ritual was imperfect and temporal.

* * *

CHRIST OUR GREAT HIGH PRIEST
And what does Hebrews say about Him:

He Himself was the sacrifice – perfect and eternal
He is our priest – seated at God's right hand.
And He is our King – invested with eternal and complete authority.

The New Testament rings with the glad shout that Jesus has made the one, true, pure, immortal sacrifice, and is alive today.

He is risen! (Mark 16:6).
He ever lives to make intercession for us (Heb. 7:25).
He is alive for evermore (Rev. 1:18).
He is King of Kings, and Lord of Lords (Rev. 19:16).
He shall reign for ever and ever! (Rev. 11:15).

Doesn't this thrill you?

STUDY 6

THE TRUE TABERNACLE AND THE NEW COVENANT

QUESTIONS

DAY 1 *Hebrews 8:1-5.*
a) Verses 1 and 2 contain the main message of this letter. What is it?
b) What two Tabernacles (or tents) does verse 5 mention and which is the TRUE one?

DAY 2 *Hebrews 8:6-13; Hebrews 7:27; Jeremiah 31:31-34; Matthew 26:28.*
a) Discuss the important differences between the Old and New Covenants in relation to the law (v. 10) and forgiveness of sin (v. 12).
b) Why is there now no need for the old Levitical system? (vv. 11, 13).

DAY 3 *Hebrews 9:1-10 (refers back to Exod. chs. 25–40); Hebrews 4:16.*
a) What two things does verse 1 say about the first Covenant?
b) How often did the High Priest enter the Most Holy Place?
c) How often did the people go in? How often can we enter in?

DAY 4 *Hebrews 9:8-15; Matthew 27:51; Hebrews 10:20.*
a) How long had people to keep the rules of the Old Covenant? (v. 10)
b) What is said about the Old Tabernacle (tent) and the New?

DAY 5 *Hebrews 9:11-14, esp. verses 12 and 14; 1 John 1:7.*
a) These verses say two very important things about Christ's blood; what are they?
b) Why is there no longer any need for us to be overwhelmed with sin, failure, guilt, and depression?

DAY 6 *Hebrews 9:15-22; Exodus 24:6-8; Leviticus 17:11; Romans 3:21-26.*
a) Since a will is only valid when someone dies (v. 17), what does Christ's death do for us (v. 15)?
b) How do these verses show you the value that God puts on forgiveness? What is the price?
c) What is involved when we forgive somebody? Is this easy?

QUESTIONS (contd.)

DAY 7 *Hebrews 9:23-28; Mark 10:45; Romans 6:23.*
 a) What do we have to do to merit God's salvation?
 b) Can you find a warning and a promise in verse 27 and verse 28?
 c) Do you love Christ for what He has done for you and are you eager to see Him come again?

NOTES

What is a Tabernacle?
The meaning can be either 'a meeting place' or 'dwelling place'. God's glory dwelt in the Holy Place, in the midst of Israel, in the earthly Tabernacle, but with the coming of Christ, we know that 'the dwelling of God is with men' (Rev. 21:3).

The Earthly Tabernacle
The picture of the Tabernacle given in Exodus 25–40 leaves us dazzled. These rich blues and reds and gleaming gold and bronze are wonderful. God demanded perfection of workmanship too (Heb. 8:5).

Yet that magnificent veil over the Holy Place silently testified that man had no access to God. The High Priest, bearing the blood of atonement could go in, but only once a year.

The True Tabernacle
The earthly Tabernacle was but a shadow of the True (Heb. 9:11) 'not made with hands'. The rending of the veil (Matt. 27:51) showed that Christ had opened the way whereby we can enter into God's presence, with confidence (Heb. 4:16).

We have that wonderful hope that our entering in now by faith in Jesus will one day be a glorious reality (1 Cor. 2:9).

What is a Covenant?
An agreement between two parties. But in our studies the agreement carries the idea of an obligation being undertaken by one person. In Deuteronomy 7:6-8 we see God's self-imposed obligation for the reconciliation of sinners to Himself.

The Old Covenant
God's promise to Abraham (Gen. 12:2) and Moses (Exod. 6:7-8) established a covenant relationship between Himself and His people. This relationship brought an obligation to obedience (Exod. 40:5-6) and holiness (Lev. 19:2). We have seen how the whole Levitical system, however, pointed to the need of a better way that would establish men in holiness and satisfy God.

The New Covenant
Zechariah prophesied it (Luke 1:72). Paul states that it comes to both Jew and Gentile, in Christ (Gal. 3:14-16). Jesus says the new Covenant is in His blood (1 Cor. 11:25). The writer to Hebrews (9:15-17) pushes the point right home –

Christ – the Mediator of the
New Covenant

STUDY 7

JESUS THE NEW AND LIVING WAY

QUESTIONS

DAY 1 *Hebrews 10:1-4. (Read v. 2 again if possible in the Living Bible.)*
a) What three things are said here about the inadequacy of the Old Testament sacrifices?
b) Discuss what verse 2 says about the consciousness of sin.

DAY 2 *Hebrews 10:5-10; Psalm 40:6-8; Hosea 6:6.*
a) Since those sacrifices weren't sufficient, what did God propose to do?
b) Did Jesus fulfil God's requirements?
c) Discuss what Christ's sacrifice has done for us (v. 10).

DAY 3 *Hebrews 10:11-14; Psalm 110:1; Hebrews 1:13.*
a) Describe the priests' position before the altar (v. 11) and Christ's position in Heaven (v. 12).
b) List the things Christ's perfect sacrifice accomplished.

DAY 4 *Hebrews 10:15-18; Jeremiah 31:31-34; Romans 5:11.*
a) What does God say that proves He is satisfied with Christ's offering?
b) What should every believer be doing and why?

DAY 5 *Hebrews 10:19-25; Hebrews 4:14-16.*
a) Can you find three important encouragements made possible for us by Christ's work? (vv. 22, 23 and 24)
b) Discuss the importance of Christian fellowship.

DAY 6 *Hebrews 10:26-31; 2 Peter 2:21 (Deuteronomy 17:2-7 will help).*
Read these verses several times in different translations and put into your own words what the Holy Spirit communicates to you.

DAY 7 *Hebrews 10:32-39.*
a) Despite any trials we may face what are we to do and why? (v. 35).
b) Describe the two choices given in verse 39. Which one are you making?

NOTES

What do we find in Hebrews Chapter 10?

CONTRASTS!
The OLD WAY	The NEW WAY vv. 9, 20
The LAW	The GOSPEL v. 1, 16
The SHADOW	The REALITY v. 1, 16
The IMPERFECT	The PERFECT v. 1, 14
MANY SACRIFICES	ONE SACRIFICE vv. 3, 4, 10, 12
The FAITHLESS	The FAITHFUL vv. 35, 36, 39

CHRIST!
INCARNATE	BORN to DIE vv. 5-10
SEATED IN GLORY	RAISED to REIGN vv. 11-13
COMING AGAIN	JUDGE AND KING v. 37

CAUTION!
WARNED against
- apostasy vv. 26-31
- wilful sin v. 26
- certain judgment if we disobey v. 27
- penalty of breaking law and far more, of spurning Christ v. 29
- coming judgment of God v. 30
- awfulness of falling into hands of the Living God v. 31

COUNSEL!
ENCOURAGED
- to draw near vv. 19-22
- to hold fast v. 23
- to show practical love v. 24
- to enjoy blessings of fellowship v. 25
- to remember how past persecution was overcome vv. 32-34
- to be bold v. 35
- to be patient vv. 35-37
- to be faithful v. 38
- to be steadfast v. 39

STUDY 8

'NOW FAITH IS BEING SURE ...' (NIV)

QUESTIONS

Use as many translations as possible.

DAY 1 Hebrews 11:1, 2; Hebrews 10:38, 39.
a) What is said about faith in verses 38 and 39?
b) Does verse 1 say 'seeing is believing' or 'believing is seeing'?

DAY 2 Hebrews 11:3; Psalm 33:6-9 (read Genesis 1 for further help).
a) How do we know God made everything?
b) Since He created everything (and everyone!) how should this affect my attitude to Him?

DAY 3 Hebrews 11:4-7; Genesis 4:3-5; Genesis 5:21-24; Genesis 6:5-22.
a) What pleased God about Abel (v. 4), Enoch (v. 5) and Noah (v. 7)?
b) What kind of pressures would Noah have been up against when he built the ark?
c) Do you find your circumstances a hindrance to your faith?

DAY 4 Hebrews 11:8-16; Genesis 11:30; Romans 4:16-22.
a) What proved that Abraham had faith?
b) Why did Sarah believe for such an impossible thing? (v. 11)
c) Would you say there is evidence today of Sarah and Abraham's faith? (v. 12 and see Gen. 15:2-6)

DAY 5 Hebrews 11:17-22; Genesis 27:33; Genesis 48:21; Genesis 50:24.
a) Why did Abraham not feel God was inconsistent in asking him to sacrifice Isaac?
b) Discuss how Isaac, Jacob and Joseph expressed their faith.

DAY 6 Hebrews 11:23-31; Exodus 2:1-3; Joshua 2:9-11; Joshua 6:15-21.
a) Why did Moses' parents (v. 23), Moses (vv. 27, 28), the Israelites (vv. 29, 30), Rahab (v. 31) act as they did?
b) Why did the pagan Rahab believe in God? (Joshua 2:10, 11)
c) Why did Moses not regret leaving the riches of Egypt?

QUESTIONS (contd.)

DAY 7 *Hebrews 11:32-40; Hebrews 12:22-24.*
a) Verses 33-38 give a tremendous list of victories won by men of faith (v. 32), right up till New Testament times. Why do you think the events of verses 33-34 and the dreadful happenings of verses 35-38 are all listed as triumphs?
b) What do you think the promise refers to in verse 39?
c) Why did these heroes not live to see it?

NOTES

ARE YOU SURE?
Jesus 'carries out and fulfils all of God's promises, no matter how many of them there are; and we have told everyone how faithful he is, giving glory to his name' (2 Cor. 1:20, LB).

'...the Gentiles are fellow heirs, members of the same body, and partakers of the promise in Christ Jesus through the gospel' (Eph. 3:6, RSV).

When you *became sure* that Christ's promise of salvation was for you, you believed.

Your continuing Christian walk and development consists of your becoming sure of every promised provision made for you in Christ.

GOD'S PROMISE
'Now if we are children, then we are heirs – heirs of God and co-heirs with Christ' (Rom. 8:17, NIV).

'So you are no longer a slave, but a son, and since you are a son, God has made you also an heir' (Gal. 4:7, NIV).

God made a covenant with Abraham, and Hebrews 11 is a living record of the living faith of Abraham and all the successive generations who were sure of God's promises and as a result God accomplished His purposes through them.

HOW SURE ARE YOU?
Do you make God's promises actual and real in your life because you believe them and act upon them? Let's take another look at Hebrews 11:1 and ask God to sweep away the cobwebs of doubt and make us the kind of people who *always are sure of His Word*.

TITLE DEEDS
The word 'substance' (AV) in verse 1 in Greek means 'title deeds'. Used in legal documents it provided the legal basis for evidence of ownership. Now, if you are included in someone's will, it could be that there is a document filed away which will make you heir to a property or fortune. You won't enter into your inheritance until your benefactor dies and the will becomes effective – but it is a legal fact that you are an heir.

Thus, verse 1 could be written, 'God has put His signature to our spiritual inheritance. Though we cannot actually see it, yet by taking God at His Word (faith) we can claim it, because the title deeds are ours.'

REALITY
Our Benefactor has already died, the will has been read, the inheritance divided. God's Word has been given; do we accept it (Heb. 9:15, 16)? Have we claimed our inheritance? It is wonderful to be secure in the knowledge that He saves us and will keep us until we enter into our Heavenly inheritance.

'... No eye has seen, no ear has heard, no mind has conceived what God has prepared for those who love Him – but God has revealed it to us by His Spirit.' (1 Cor. 2:9, 10).

STUDY 9

A FAITH THAT FUNCTIONS AND NEVER GIVES UP

QUESTIONS

DAY 1 *Hebrews 12:1-11; Mark 8:34-38.*
a) Read verses 1-3 and discuss the two great encouragements we have in the Christian faith?
b) Why does God permit suffering in a Christian's life?

DAY 2 *Hebrews 12:12-17; Isaiah 35:3, 4; Romans 15:1, 2; Deuteronomy 29:18.*
a) Why are we to throw off despondency and face life with courage and confidence?
b) Discuss what could result from 'a root of bitterness' (v. 15) in your life.

DAY 3 *Hebrews 12:18-24.*
a) Refer back to Deuteronomy 4:11-13; Exodus 19:12, 13; 20:18, 19. Because God's holy presence so terrified the Israelites what did they ask Moses to do?
b) What is the difference in our approach to God today?

DAY 4 *Hebrews 12:25-29; Hebrews 1:1, 2; Mark 13:31; 2 Peter 3:7.*
a) God's voice literally shook the earth at Sinai so the people couldn't avoid what He said. Why can we not evade God's voice? (Ps. 139:7-12)
b) Why are we to be thankful and worship God? (vv. 28, 29 and see also Dan. 2:44 and 2 Pet. 3:9-14.)

DAY 5 *Hebrews 13:1-6; Deuteronomy 31:6; Joshua 1:5; Psalm 118:6; Psalm 89:1.*
a) List qualities that should be evident in a Christian's life.
b) In what are we to be confident? What have we to declare? (vv. 5, 6)

DAY 6 *Hebrews 13:7-16; Hebrews 12:2.*
a) What do verses 7-10 teach us?
b) Can you state a Christian's duty and a leader's responsibility from verses 7 and 17?

QUESTIONS (contd.)

DAY 7 *Hebrews 13:18-25; Colossians 2:12; Ephesians 1:19, 20; 1 John 5:4.*
    a) What power raised Jesus from the dead?
    b) What power operates in each Christian?
    c) What enables God's power to be effective in our lives?

NOTES

Did the heroes of faith in Hebrews 11 have a BIG FAITH? We are not told, but Scripture reveals that they had a BIG GOD! Jesus told His disciples that their faith should be able to MOVE MOUNTAINS (Matt. 21:19-22). And to do that their faith had to be as big as a mustard seed! (Luke 17:6).

All His life Jesus expressed His absolute confidence in God by His perfect obedience to Him (Phil. 2:8). When we study the life of Moses we find out that unbelief and disobedience go hand in hand. Hebrews 11 shows us clearly that faith and obedience go together. It gives us many examples of those whose faith in God spurred them to action.

FAITH WORKS!
Abel made a righteous offering; Enoch walked pleasing to God; Noah acted on God's word; Abraham obeyed God; Abraham and Sarah believed God; Isaac blessed Jacob; Jacob worshipped God and blessed Joseph's sons; Joseph gave instructions about his burial in Canaan, all long before there was anything visible to support their actions; Moses refused Egypt's riches, anticipating a spiritual inheritance; Rahab was saved physically and spiritually because she confessed Israel's God (Heb. 11).

FAITH TRIUMPHS!
Subdues kingdoms, works righteousness, obtains promises, stops lions' mouths, quenches fire, avoids the sword, is mighty in battle, routs armies, endures torture, bears trials, suffers persecution, torture, deprivation, loneliness, loss of goods, death (Heb. 11).

FAITH NEVER GIVES UP!
Because God never gives up on us! 'Never will I leave you; never will I forsake you.' Do we say with confidence 'The Lord is my helper; I will not be afraid. What can man do to me'? (Heb. 13:5, 6, NIV).

HOW BIG IS YOUR GOD?
His almighty power which raised Jesus from the dead (Heb. 13:20) works in us (Eph. 3:20) so that we may eternally triumph over sin, resist temptation (Heb. 2:18) withstand the pull of the world (1 John 2:17) and resist the devil's onslaughts (Rev. 12:11).

Paul says 'I have been sent to bring FAITH to those God has chosen and to teach them to know God's truth – the kind of truth that CHANGES lives – so that they can have ETERNAL LIFE which GOD promised them before the world began – and he CANNOT LIE! (Titus 1:1, 2 LB).

This is the VICTORY ... even our (your) FAITH (1 John 5:4).

STUDY 10
QUESTIONS

DAY 1 *Hebrews 1:1-3.*
List the things these verses tell us about our wonderful Lord. Now take each one separately and ask yourself, 'What difference would it make to me if this were not so?'

DAY 2 *Hebrews 2:1-4.*
List the following 'Do's and Don'ts'.
WARNING 1
   DO ... (v. 1) DON'T ... (v. 1) DO ... (vv. 1-4)
WARNING 2 – *Hebrews 3:7-13.*
   DO ... (v. 7) DON'T ... (v. 8) DON'T ... (v. 12) DO ... (v. 13)

DAY 3 WARNING 3 – *Hebrews 4:7-11*
   DO (v. 11).
When does God want us to enjoy His rest? (2 Cor. 6:2)
WARNING 4 – *Hebrews 6:1.*
   DON'T ... (v. 1) DO ... (v. 1)

DAY 4 WARNING 5 – *Hebrews 10:19-25.*
   DO ... (v. 22) DO ... (v. 23) DO ... (v. 24) DO ... (v. 25).
WARNING 6 – *Hebrews 12:25-29.*
   DON'T ... (v. 25) DO ... (v. 28)

DAY 5 WARNING 7 – *Hebrews 13:7-13.*
   DO ... (v. 7) DON'T ... (v. 9) DO ... (v. 13)
What is our encouragement when tempted to give in? (Heb. 2:18)

DAY 6 *Hebrews 13:20, 21.*
Was this prayer for us as well as those early Hebrew Christians? Does it encourage you that Christ is praying like this for us now? (Heb. 7:25)
Do you see how the prayer sums up much of what we have learned in Hebrews?
Our God of Peace – because Christ reconciled us to God.
Our Risen Saviour – Jesus, whom God raised from the dead.
Our Constant Shepherd – Jesus, the Shepherd of the sheep.

QUESTIONS (contd.)

DAY 6 (contd.)
   Our Everlasting Covenant – sealed by the blood of Jesus.
   Our Personal Sanctification – which God work in us.
   Our Motivation for Service – God perfecting us to do His Will.
   Our Spontaneous Praise – God alone is worthy.

DAY 7 *TO HELP YOU UNDERSTAND AND REMEMBER THE TEACHING IN HEBREWS*

GOD'S CONCERN

    CHRIST'S PROVISION

        SPIRIT'S OPERATION

            CHRISTIANS' PRIVILEGE

        SERVICE (Eph. 6:5-8) (Heb. 9:14)

      SANCTIFICATION (I Pet. 1:2)

    SALVATION (Heb. 5:9)

SINFULNESS (Isa. 59:2)

Look up the references under each column.

NOTES

Four keywords stand out in this wonderful study. Let us look at them as we come to the end.

Keyword 1. PERFECT
Read the references and fill in the missing words.

> God is .... (Matt. 5:48)
> Jesus was made .... (Heb. 2:9, 10)
> I am not yet .... (Phil. 3:12, 13)

The word 'perfect' is used fourteen times in Hebrews.
When applied to Christ and His work it means 'perfectly completed'.
When applied to Christians it implies 'in process of being made complete'.

Let us then go on to perfection (maturity) (Heb. 6:1) for He who began the good work in us will bring it to COMPLETION in the day of Christ (Phil. 1:6).

Keyword 2. ETERNAL
What a list Hebrews gives us of eternal things! The Son, Priest, King, New Covenant, judgment, redemption, salvation, inheritance, glory – all ETERNAL.
ETERNAL LIFE! God planned it. Christ brought it.
What is it (Rom. 6:22-23)? Who has it (John 11:25-27)?
Assurance of Salvation should fill our hearts with praise. Won't it be wonderful to join with all the mighty company of God's children in heaven and sing –

> 'Worthy is the Lamb who was slain
> To receive power and wealth and wisdom and might
> And honour and glory and blessing!
> To Him Who sits upon the throne and to the Lamb
> Be blessing and honour and glory and might
>   FOR EVER AND EVER!' (Rev. 5:12, 13, RSV)

Keyword 3. BETTER
There is no doubt about it! We never had it better!
The old 'shadow' covenant is completely wiped out by the reality of the new one.
Let's list all the BETTER things mentioned and chase away the last trace of unbelief.

CHRIST – better than angels.
BLESSER – better than the blessed.

CHRISTIANS – have a better hope.
SALVATION – produces better fruit.
CHRIST'S PRIESTHOOD – is better than Aaron's.
NEW COVENANT – better than the old.
CHRISTIANS – established on better promises.
CHRIST'S SACRIFICE – a better sacrifice.
HEAVEN – better than the world.
SPIRITUAL RESURRECTION – better than physical resurrection.
BLOOD OF NEW COVENANT – better than old.
HEAVENLY INHERITANCE – better than a temporal one.

Phew ... it's beyond human comprehension. How can anyone miss the BETTER WAY into such an inheritance? (John 14:6).
And the best has yet to be! (See I Cor. 2:9, 10.)

Keyword 4. PARTAKERS
Partakers, Sharers. Having all things in common. Being partners. Fellow-partakers.
Receiving salvation we become:

- Partakers of the goods things of God.
- Partakers of Christ.
- Partakers of the Holy Spirit.

ANSWER GUIDE

The following pages contain an Answer Guide. It is recommended that answers to the questions be attempted before turning to this guide. It is only a guide and the answers given should not be treated as exhaustive.

GUIDE TO INTRODUCTORY STUDY

The purpose of the starter discussion is to help your group to identify with the kind of problems the first century Christians had. Encourage people to participate on the ordinary, everyday level; perhaps share times when these things have been a stumbling block to them. This calls for frankness and openness, and a willingness to share problems.

The references are progressive – slow to understand, discouraged, lost initial enthusiasm, failed to grow, neglected worship, disloyal to leaders, easily led astray, in danger of giving up their faith.

HEBREWS 1:1-3.
Encourage sharing and refer to as many instances as possible where God spoke prior to Christ's birth.

    e.g.   through dreams (Gen. 28:12-16).
            to the patriarchs (Gen. 12:1-2; Exod. 3:1-6, 14; Josh 1:1-9).
            through prophets (Amos 3:1).
            by angels (Luke 1:26-28).

Creation and nature speak to us of a Creator God. They indicate that He is wonderful, powerful, original, kind, generous, beauty-loving, etc. Because He made us, He is wiser and greater than we are, but He seems to be very far away (see Jer. 23:23).

He has spoken by His Son – this is the most revealing communication man has ever had.

He shows us His character in its completeness (see John 14:9), and tells us how much He cares for us as individuals (John 3:16).

Remember to ask people next week to quote Chapter 4:14, from memory, if possible. Be sure to learn it yourself!

Bibliography:

The New Bible Commentary (Inter-Varsity Fellowship)
Hebrews Tyndale New Testament Commentary (Hewitt)
We Would See Jesus (Hession)
Holiest of All (Andrew Murray)
Way into the Holiest (F. B. Meyer)
Jesus Christ, Prophet and Priest (Andrew Murray)
(You may be able to borrow some of these from your minister or church library.)

GUIDE TO STUDY 1

DAY 1   a) Angels worship the Son, are messengers, servants; do not reign beside God; help and care for those whom Christ will save.
b) The Lord is the Son of God, is honoured of God, is worthy of worship, is King of an eternal Kingdom, loves righteousness and hates evil, God's special favour rests of Him, He is Creator of the Universe, is eternal, unchangeable, will create a new Universe, sits exalted at God's right hand.
c) How vastly superior the Son is to angels.

DAY 2   a) He never changes. What God declared in the Old, He perfectly fulfils in the New.
b) Personal. (e.g. promises given in the Bible are true for me today. Jesus' character in the N.T. exactly matches what I personally know Him to be like.)

DAY 3   a) Those who would inherit life in Christ.
b) Not to neglect God's offer of salvation.

DAY 4   a) We have a greater responsibility to respond than those who received the message from angels.
b) It was announced by the Lord, confirmed to us by those who heard Him, and attested to by God's miracles.

DAY 5   a) No.
b) God meant him to rule the universe.

DAY 6   a) Christ was not created like the angels, but as Son of God He became also Son of Man, born of a woman, to identify with our humanity.
b) So that He could defeat the devil, who holds the power of death.
c) Humility, confession and repentance before God is the key.

DAY 7   Brings us to God (v. 10), makes us holy (v. 11), makes us realize God is our Father and he has made us His kinsmen (v. 11), breaks Satan's hold on us (v. 14), brings us deliverance from fear and death (v. 15), makes Him an eternal high priest for us (v. 17), brings us succour in temptation (v. 18).

GUIDE TO STUDY 2

DAY 1   a) The people of God are His house, His dwelling place. (N.B. A church building is not, in the Scriptural sense, God's house.)
b) God Himself.

DAY 2   a) A servant is under orders, preparing things for his master. A son owns everything and uses things for his own purposes.
b) Moses was the servant, Christ the Son.
c) We must hold on with courage and hope to our faith. (Remember the Introductory Study?)

DAY 3   a) Discussion.
b) Their hearts were not right; they were frightened and forgot to trust God.
c) Today.

DAY 4   a) Easy, restful, with no battles to fight.
b) The people in the land appeared much more powerful than they.
c) Unbelief.

DAY 5   a) His rest (i.e., inward peace whatever the outward circumstances).
b) If we fail to believe the gospel or receive Jesus Christ.

DAY 6   a) Don't harden your hearts; don't disobey God.
b) Resisting God's love, not being willing to surrender our wills.

DAY 7   a) We must make an effort to live as God wants us to; be careful about disobedience; remember God sees everything; hold on firmly to our faith.
b) 1. Christ is God, Moses was a human servant. Christ brought the new law of love, Moses brought O.T. Law.
2. It is living and active, and when we read it, it has power to break us or to uplift us.

GUIDE TO STUDY 3

DAY 1 a) Himself, the believers of his day, and all who since then have put their faith in Christ.
b) At the Father's right hand, in the very presence of God.
c) Jesus is our forerunner, He has gone before us on our behalf.

DAY 2 a) He refused the devil's suggestions on the grounds of God's Word.
b) He sympathizes, because He has known the same trials and temptations in His earthly life, and He bore our very sins on the Cross.

DAY 3 a) With confidence, without fear.
b) On the grounds of Christ's finished work, that we may draw all we need from Him.

DAY 4 a) God.
b) To represent the people before God, making sacrifices for their sin.
c) Because, being a man, he sinned too.

DAY 5 a) God.
b) To provide a sacrifice for sin and mediate between God and man.
c) He offered one sacrifice for sin forever, and lives forever to make intercession for His people.

DAY 6 a) He was subject to His parents, walked in continual obedience to His Father and humbled Himself to become our Redeemer.
b) We need and will receive correction and chastisement from God that we may learn to walk in obedience, love and trust.

DAY 7 Let the group read the Scriptures around, then read the following extract:

'O Father, must I drink this cup? My soul is exceedingly sorrowful. It's not so much the cross, the crown of thorns, the mocking, the physical pain, But the aloneness, the weight of sin and guilt, the separation from You. Nevertheless Father, Not My Will, but Thine be done That others may live.'

Without comment, have one or two pray and thank the Lord for His overcoming work on our behalf.

GUIDE TO STUDY 4

DAY 1 a) 1. They feed on milk, haven't learned to use their minds.
2. They can eat solid food and should have 'trained' minds.
b) Christians may initially need feeding and help, but should go on to understand, and to be able to teach the Word of God to others. Beware of retarded growth. Lay a foundation then build on it!
c) 'There is much to say about the priesthood of Melchizedek, but it is difficult to teach those who are lazy (sluggish) Christians.'

DAY 2 a) Hebrews 6:2 – basic doctrines of baptism, consecration, resurrection, eternal judgment.
b) God's plan is that we should grow in our spiritual life, desiring to become like Christ, learning to not only understand, but to be teachers of His Word.

DAY 3 a) All crossed the Red Sea, but only some went into Canaan.
b) It is possible after being taught the truth to stubbornly reject it and miss out on the eternal blessing God offers us.

DAY 4 a) Accept or reject.
b) For those who reject it, even if they appear to be good and go along with Christian principles, their lives will bear no fruit and in the end they will be judged and condemned.
For those who receive the salvation of God, their lives will reveal 'the things that accompany salvation' (seen in the next few verses) and will 'inherit the promises', i.e. inherit Heaven and all the benefits of being a Christian.

DAY 5 a) Faith, hope, love.
b) Faith, hope, love.
c) An exhortation to continuing faith and patient persevering in the Christian life.

DAY 6 a) By the swearing of an oath (or giving a pledge).
b) He believed God implicitly.
c) People feel an oath brings in a third party (God?) who can ensure the word given will be kept.

DAY 7 a) The hope of salvation and eternal life.
b) The living Lord Jesus Christ in heaven on our behalf.
c) The certainty of the hope of salvation and eternal life.

GUIDE TO STUDY 5

DAY 1 a) The comparison between Christ and Melchizedek.
b) He was a king and a priest. Abraham met him, received a blessing, and gave him one tenth of his everything.

DAY 2 a) King – of Salem, of Justice, of Peace; Priest of God, Priest forever; Blesser of Abraham; Superior to Abraham; Superior to Levitical priests (7:9); no record of birth, or death.
b) King. Priest. Eternal.

DAY 3 a) They were memorials and thanksgivings for God-given victories.
b) Christ's eternal victory over sin.

DAY 4 a) The one who blesses.
b) Every spiritual blessing. This includes all that the grace, gifts and love of God has given us in Christ. Redemption and forgiveness are part of this.

DAY 5 a) Gratefulness to God for His deliverances.
b) By the tithes of the people.
c) God.
d) See I Corinthians 16:2. (Tithing is no substitute for disobedience in other areas of our lives.) Scripture says 'The Lord loveth a cheerful giver. Surely our response to Him should be a glad yielding of all we have and are. Tithing is a good beginning. See Malachi 3:8-12 and I Samuel 15:22.

DAY 6 a) They could not give perfection – God must have a better way to deal fully and finally with sin.
b) Aaron and the Levites were human and finite. Their sins, like those of the people, had to be atoned for. Aaron (unlike Melchizedek) died. God's plan of salvation for mankind included the Levites.

DAY 7 Emphasis could be put on the words, 'perfect for ever' (7:28, NIV). Christ is now King (Rev. 1:5) and Priest forever (Heb. 6:20) and as His redeemed ones we are made Kings (Rev. 1:6) and Priests (I Pet. 2:5). N.B. Some translations (e.g., NIV) indicate Revelation 1:6 to refer to 'a kingdom' instead of kings

GUIDE TO STUDY 6

DAY 1 a) Our High Priest fulfils God's standard of priesthood and mediates between God and man and the new Covenant (salvation through Christ's atonement) from the heavenly Tabernacle (the very Presence of God).
b) The old Levitical Tabernacle, and the True Heavenly one.

DAY 2 a) The old was an outward imposition of the written law demanding the constant bringing of sacrifices for sin. The new is from the heart, changed and responsive through Christ, and dependent upon Him, our eternal sacrifice for sin.
b) The old temporary system is done away with through Christ's eternal sacrifice and priesthood.

DAY 3 a) It had regulations of worship and an earthly meeting place.
b) Once a year.
c) Never. As often as we need, confident in Christ, our Redeemer.

DAY 4 a) Till Christ, the mediator of the new Covenant would appear (v. 11 onwards).
b) *The Old*: temporary (v. 8), offerings and ritual continual (v. 10), the priest imperfect (v. 9), forgiveness incomplete (v. 9).
The New: eternal, not man-made (v. 11), perfect offering (v. 12), perfect, eternal priest (v. 15), perfect forgiveness (v. 14).

DAY 5 a) His blood makes us acceptable with God forever (v. 12) and makes us fit to serve God (v. 14).
b) Because the blood continually cleanses all that is brought to Jesus for cleansing.

DAY 6 a) Ushers us into our inheritance (Rom. 8:17).
b) Blood was the price of forgiveness in the Old Testament pattern, but the supreme price for our eternal salvation is the blood of the Son of God.
c) To forgive I have to break, humble myself, suffer death to my pride. Human nature does not find this easy.

DAY 7 a) Absolutely nothing. Salvation is a gift of God (Rom. 6:23).
b) Man must face judgment when he dies – a warning to be ready. There is no dread in Christ's second coming for the believer because of God's promise of salvation.
c) Personal.

GUIDE TO STUDY 7

DAY 1 a) Since they were only a foreshadow of the real thing to come these sacrifices:
  a. Could never make the one who offered them perfect.
  b. Had to be repeated again and again.
  c. Were powerless to take away sin.
b) If the blood of animals had effectively dealt with sin and guilt there would have been no need to repeat them.

DAY 2 a) God contemplated a better sacrifice (vv. 6-9).
b) Yes (v. 9).
c) Makes us holy. Those who are redeemed by Christ once again become God-centred instead of self-centred.

DAY 3 a) The priests stand – denoting a continuous work. Christ sits – His work is finished, perfectly completed.
b) It cancelled out the old, ineffective system of the law; it brought us forgiveness and cleansing from sin, once and for all; it qualified Christ to sit at God's right hand; it made all believers perfect in the sight of God.

DAY 4 a) Verse 17: He no longer remembers our sins or lawless deeds.
b) Rejoicing in God because of what Christ has done (Rom. 5:11) and obeying God because He has put His law in their hearts (Heb. 10:16).

DAY 5 a) 'Let us draw near ...'; 'Let us hold unswervingly (fast) ...'; 'Let us consider one another ...'.
b) Very important (v. 25) especially as the day of the Lord's return draws near, so that we can encourage each other.

DAY 6 Discussion should bring out the seriousness of wilful sin against light, and the rejection of Christ's offer of salvation. If, under the Old Covenant idolaters had to suffer death, how much under the New Covenant should deliberate rejection of Christ bring the judgment of God?

DAY 7 a) Persevere. We need to remember the glorious hope of an eternity with Christ, don't be discouraged or deterred from faithfully following Him now.
b) We can be unbelieving and miss out on salvation or keep believing and press on into an eternal inheritance.
Personal.

GUIDE TO STUDY 8

DAY 1 a) By having faith in God we have salvation, or eternal life; conversely, by refusing to believe we perish.
b) 'Believing is seeing'.

DAY 2 a) By faith – by believing God (v. 3).
b) Personal – (I know Him to be a powerful, creative God, and I can safely trust my life to Him.)

DAY 3 a) Their faith which: enabled Abel to make the right sacrifice, Enoch to walk pleasing to God, Noah to be obedient.
b) People would have scorned him for building a ship on dry land.
c) Personal – but public opinion and circumstances could easily sway us.

DAY 4 a) In obedience to God he left all that was familiar and moved into the unknown. He accepted God's promises.
b) Because of God's promises to them. (See Gen. 15:1-6; 17:16; 18:9-14.)
c) Yes. Not only the proliferation of Jews, but also of Abraham's spiritual heirs (us? and all the Church of God) shows that God is fulfilling His promise (Rom. 4:16, 17).

DAY 5 a) He knew God would fulfil His promise of giving him descendants through Isaac even if it meant raising him from the dead.
b) Isaac, although he had a natural liking for Esau, believed God would fulfil His promise through Jacob (Gen. 27:33). Jacob and Joseph looked beyond their own deaths and anticipated the move from Egypt to Canaan (Gen. 48:21 and 50:24).

DAY 6 a) Because they believed God.
b) Rahab believed because she had seen and heard how God had delivered His children from the Egyptians.
c) Because he believed God had something better for him ahead.

DAY 7 a) Because all were *victories* of faith.
b) The climax of His eternal plan – sending His Son to redeem mankind.
c) God planned that many in succeeding generations would have a part in it too.

GUIDE TO STUDY 9

DAY 1   a) The example of Christian witness past and present and above all, the Lord Jesus who has triumphed over Satan and Sin.
b) His chastening hand on us assures us we are His children and just as parental discipline results in temporal benefits for our children, so God's testings and trials produce godly qualities in us (v. 10).

DAY 2   a) Because inconsistency and faint-heartedness can discourage others who are not so strong in their faith.
b) Bitterness harms my own personal life, spreads to others and can lead to apostasy (instanced by Esau who gave away his inheritance to indulge his appetite (v. 16).)

DAY 3   a) Speak to them instead of God (Exod. 20:18, 19).
b) Through Christ we can draw near to God with confidence (Heb. 4:16). Read Hebrews 12:18-24 in the Living Bible to get the contrast between Sinai and Heaven.

DAY 4   a) The Bible says we cannot get away from God (Ps. 139:7-12).
b) For He has delivered us from the wrath of His judgment of sin, made provision for us to serve Him in holiness and made us partakers of an eternal Kingdom.

DAY 5   a) Love, hospitality, concern and care for others, contentment, cheerfulness (and note the reference to God-honouring marriage relationships).
b) God's presence and promises. God's faithfulness.

DAY 6   a) Don't be perverted from a true Christian walk by joining in useless rituals of eating and worship; take to heart what faithful men have taught you and remember our true altar (Jesus Christ, His cross and sacrifice) in which unbelievers have no part; and Jesus Christ (the sustainer of our teachers) who never changes (and therefore will be our sustainer too).
b) Christians – respect and learn from leaders. Leaders – teach as those accountable to God.

DAY 7   a) God's power.
b) God's power.
c) Our believing His word, i.e., FAITH.

GUIDE TO STUDY 10

DAY 1

God spoke through Him	– I would not have that revelation of what God was like.
He is heir of all things	– I would not be a joint-heir with Him.
He made the universe	– Jesus would not have been one with God.
He is the exact likeness of God	– He would have been like sinful man.
He sustains the universe	– Life could not go on.
He died to cleanse men from sin	– I would still be unforgiven.
He sits at God's right hand	– I would have no eternal hope.

DAY 2

1. DO watch out. DON'T drift. DO avail yourself of God's provision.
2. DO listen to God's voice today. DON'T harden your heart. DON'T turn away from God. DO encourage one another.

DAY 3

3. DO apply yourself to enter into God's rest. NOW.
4. DON'T stick around in the ABC of your faith. DO go on to be a strong Christian.

DAY 4

5. DO draw near to God. DO hold strongly to Christ your hope. DO stimulate others to love and positive helpfulness. DO meet together and encourage each other.
6. DON'T refuse to listen to God.
Be thankful and worship God in a way that is acceptable to Him (NIV).
Please God by serving Him with thankful hearts (LB).

DAY 5

7. DO remember your leaders, and imitate their faith. DON'T be led astray by unscriptural teaching. DO identify with Christ, heedless of the cost.
We know that Jesus can give us the strength to overcome temptation. He is the overcomer – He dwells in our hearts.

DAY 6

'Yes' to all questions.

THE WORD WORLDWIDE

We first heard of WORD WORLDWIDE over 20 years ago when Marie Dinnen, its founder, shared excitedly about the wonderful way ministry to one needy woman had exploded to touch many lives. It was great to see the Word of God being made central in the lives of thousands of men and women, then to witness the life-changing results of them applying the Word to their circumstances. Over the years the vision for WORD WORLDWIDE has not dimmed in the hearts of those who are involved in this ministry. God is still at work through His Word and in today's self-seeking society, the Word is even more relevant to those who desire true meaning and purpose in life. WORD WORLDWIDE is a ministry of WEC International, an interdenominational missionary society, whose sole purpose is to see Christ known, loved and worshipped by all, particularly those who have yet to hear of His wonderful name. This ministry is a vital part of our work and we warmly recommend the WORD WORLDWIDE 'Geared for Growth' Bible studies to you. We know that as you study His Word you will be enriched in your personal walk with Christ. It is our hope that as you are blessed through these studies, you will find opportunities to help others discover a personal relationship with Jesus. As a mission we would encourage you to work with us to make Christ known to the ends of the earth.

Stewart and Jean Moulds – British Directors, **WEC International**.

A full list of over 50 'Geared for Growth' studies can be obtained from:

ENGLAND *North East/South*: John and Ann Edwards
5 Louvaine Terrace, Hetton-le-Hole, Tyne & Wear, DH5 9PP
Tel. 0191 5262803 Email: rhysjohn.edwards@virgin.net
North West/Midlands: Anne Jenkins
2 Windermere Road, Carnforth, Lancs., LA5 9AR
Tel. 01524 734797 Email: anne@jenkins.abelgratis.com
West: Pam Riches Tel. 01594 834241

IRELAND Steffney Preston
33 Harcourts Hill, Portadown, Craigavon, N. Ireland, BT62 3RE
Tel. 028 3833 7844 Email: sa.preston@talk21.com

SCOTLAND Margaret Halliday
10 Douglas Drive, Newton Mearns, Glasgow, G77 6HR
Tel. 0141 639 8695 Email: mhalliday@onetel.net.uk

WALES William and Eirian Edwards
Penlan Uchaf, Carmarthen Road, Kidwelly, Carms., SA17 5AF
Tel. 01554 890423 Email: penlanuchaf@fwi.co.uk

UK CO-ORDINATOR

Anne Jenkins
2 Windermere Road, Carnforth, Lancs., LA5 9AR
Tel. 01524 734797 Email: anne@jenkins.abelgratis.com

UK Website: www.gearedforgrowth.co.uk

Christian Focus Publications
publishes books for all ages

Our mission statement –
STAYING FAITHFUL
In dependence upon God we seek to help make His infallible word, the Bible, relevant. Our aim is to ensure that the Lord Jesus Christ is presented as the only hope to obtain forgiveness of sin, live a useful life and look forward to heaven with Him.
REACHING OUT
Christ's last command requires us to reach out to our world with His gospel. We seek to help fulfill that by publishing books that point people towards Jesus and help them develop a Christ-like maturity. We aim to equip all levels of readers for life, work, ministry and mission.

Books in our adult range are published in three imprints.
Christian Focus contains popular works including biographies, commentaries, basic doctrine, and Christian living. Our children's books are also published in this imprint.
Mentor focuses on books written at a level suitable for Bible College and seminary students, pastors, and other serious readers; the imprint includes commentaries, doctrinal studies, examination of current issues, and church history.
Christian Heritage contains classic writings from the past.